The Black Ostrich

Dr. Charles Kibaara Nyaga(ED. D ,
M. DIV., AAT)

Dedication

I dedicate this book to all the individuals whose constant support and compassion have drastically impacted my journey.

I would like to spare a moment to thank Mr. Charles H. Kuck, whose expertise guided me through the complex US Immigration system. I am immensely grateful to Rev. George Tatro for his friendship with me and my refugee friends in Clarkston, Georgia, and his relentless advocacy for marginalized families. Special thanks to Rev. Gad Mpoyo of Shalom International in Stone Mountain, Georgia. Your warm fellowship and tireless efforts in seeking 'Shalom' for refugees in the USA have left an indelible mark on my heart. Finally, I am thankful to Doris Mukangu and Reggie Erawoc of Amani Women's Center. Their dedication to 'Stitching' together the shattered lives of refugee women after their harrowing journeys across countless borders and capitals is nothing short of inspiring.

This book is a tribute to all these individuals who have had a heartfelt impact on my story and the lives of so many others.

Acknowledgment

There are many people to acknowledge for being my "traveling companions" on this journey. I feel, however, compelled to single out some names:

The late Jan Boehm, Jackie McCown, the late Ginny, Charlie, Rev Alig, Daniel Wright, Jennifer Whitehead, Connie, and Linwood Swain-all member friends at the former Southminster Presbyterian Church (USA) in Marietta Georgia, for supporting my family during challenging times through the immigration process. Finally, I acknowledge Dr. Alicia Kay Gelford-Holtz for her genuine friendship and belief in me during my early days in the New Lands, which were instrumental in shaping my path. Your presence in my life has been a true blessing. Thank you for being my guiding light.

Table of Contents

Introduction

"Welcome To My Journey"

As we embark on an extraordinary journey together, step right into a world where laughter and touching stories intertwine. I warmly welcome you to join me for a wonderful and bumpy insight into my life over a cup of tea in this autobiography. Fasten your seatbelt as we travel through the thrilling highs and shocking lows that fermented my existence.

Hold on, though, my friend! This book dodges the conventional format and storyline that you find in other autobiographies. In fact, it's a colorful and humorous adventure that seeks to debunk myths and confront presumptions about immigrant communities. Apparently, some objectionable rumors that immigrant communities are favored by **'White'** Americans and the assumption that once any immigrant arrives in America, he or she, with his/her family, is ready to integrate into the American culture quickly are circulating among host countries. However, we are going to unveil the truth, so we can all laugh heartily about it.

We'll confute the false notion that we're all riding a magical carpet of privilege through life together, as well as examine the core of immigrant life through inspirational TRUE stories based on racism, and xenophobia.

While keeping a candid and humorous tone, this book will reveal the harsh reality of the immigrant life with vulnerability in the spotlight. You'll nod in agreement at some points, laugh at related incidents, and maybe even cry a little as I share personal experiences and lessons learned. We'll find our way through the maze of cultural conflicts, enjoy the benefits of adaptability, and form strong bonds amidst turbulence.

But this journey, dear reader, isn't about my experiences only; it's also about appreciating your own growth path and resolving the cause serving as a disconnect between immigrant cultures and host countries, especially the mistrust of refugees on their hosts for the lack of empathy in the complex navigation of the American (Western) social system. I want to encourage and equip you to appreciate your unique personality, traits, and accomplishments.

So settle in, and prepare for an exciting trip. Together, we'll debunk the myth surrounding immigrants and have an absolute ball while doing so. Get ready to enjoy the ride that is life itself as you learn, laugh, and accept it. Greetings, my friend!

Chapter One

"A Glimpse into My Childhood Part 1"

Welcome, my dear readers. Join me as we go back in time to the colorful days of my childhood. Let's take a trip down memory lane and revisit the events that shaped the person I am today—my memories, youth, and family relationships. So, grab a cozy spot as we touch down my early stages of life.

It all started in the arms of my loving parents, who were not just regular people but also passionate educators before my father joined ministry within the Presbyterian Church of East Africa (P.C.E.A.). I was no exception to their talent for instilling curiosity and a desire for knowledge in their children. I was raised in a society where education was ingrained into every aspect of daily life and was thought of as one's constant companion.

My early education was done in the surroundings of the beautiful, picturesque lands of rural Kenya by the slopes of Mount Kenya. The seeds of my dreams started to blossom in front of this gorgeous backdrop. The classroom became my haven, and the book pages became doors leading to my imagination's unexplored territories.

High school, ah! This is where I began to figure out what subject excited me as a young self. I went to a technical High School where I first encountered engineering. It was when I became fascinated by mechanics and electrical engineering. Oh, the dreams that flew in those corridors! My main desire was to become an aeronautic engineer with the now-defunct East African Airways, which served Kenya, Uganda, and Tanzania before it broke apart.

However, life had other things in store, as it frequently does. By a stroke of luck, I trained as a technical agricultural and mechanical engineering instructor before coming to the USA for higher education. I served as a frontline educator for ten years, developing young students' brains and sharing my enthusiasm for the intricate workings of technology and engineering wonders.

Later in life, taking a leap of faith, I turned my attention to the United States in search of a better education and a new chapter in my personal development.

This chapter has merely touched the surface of my life. However, the subsequent chapters will unveil my struggles as an immigrant and my battle to stay alive and thrive in this dual facet world. Moreover, we'll go further into the events that shaped the person in front of you today as a group.

So, my reader, let's bid farewell to the chapter of my childhood and head for the adventurous experiences that await us in the following chapters.

Chapter Two

"A Glimpse into My Childhood Part 2"

Not a day passed when I did not imagine the tempting possibilities of the United States. They had become ingrained in my thoughts and dreams, pulling me across the ocean to a future full of opportunities. The embers of my dreams became brighter as the years passed, creating a fire inside of me that wouldn't go out.

My attention was drawn like a siren by the stories of advanced education and the chance to immerse oneself in the complex world of engineering. My heart was drawn towards a future that seemed both unclear and promising by the urge to explore unexplored areas of knowledge. It appeared as though the aroma of change, of difficulties waiting to be overcome, and of dreams awaiting fulfillment permeated the very air.

Every morning as I awoke, I was thinking about that far-off place. Intense intellectual conversations could be almost physically felt on my skin, heard echoing across expansive lecture halls, and seen in the laboratories where novel concepts were given concrete life. The aspirations I had carefully cultivated since the hallways of my high school days were about to become a reality. Every waking moment was infused with a soft mix of anticipation and exhilaration just from thinking about it.

The dream to study in the United States was now a determined mission rather than just a simple pastime. My desire to cross the ocean and land in America became stronger with each passing day. It was a force that flowed through my veins, driving me onward and giving me the fortitude to face the obstacles in my path. Under the force of my unshakeable resolve, the walls of distance and uncertainty fell.

The dreams that had appeared to be far-off stars now glowed brightly, illuminating the path I was paving. I needed bravery to make the decision to give up the security of familiarity and embrace the unknown, but I was strengthened by my belief that this was the route I was supposed to take. My family's constant support served as a steady wind beneath my wings as they stood by my side.

My parents recognized the importance of this pursuit since they had devoted their lives to fostering curiosity and igniting the spark of education. I had their constant support throughout my life - it was like a lantern of its own. They never stopped me from achieving anything. As I prepared to confront the challenges that lay ahead of me, their sacrifices and the teachings they had taught me served as my armor.

I eventually found myself on the verge of a new chapter in my life as time passed like a river. The aspirations I had planted in the fertile soil of my early classrooms—nourished by my curiosity and tenacity—were about to come true. The legends of the United States were no longer tales of a far-off nation; instead, they were about to become the tale of my own journey—one towards increased knowledge, understanding, and personal development.

I could feel the winds of change whispering their secrets to me as the pages of my existence turned. I took a deep breath and prepared to embark on a new path that would lead me to the fulfillment of my dreams, the discovery of my potential, and the creation of my own destiny on the shores of a country that held promises that had yet to be revealed. I was filled with anticipation, and my spirit was burning with determination.

However, little did I know that when the time came, these feelings would instantly be turned into a fear of leaving everything behind and starting a new life in a foreign land. The prospect of leaving behind the comfort of familiarity and the warmth of family began to cast a shadow over the dreams that had once shone so brightly. The very determination that had propelled me forward now stood side by side with doubt and uncertainty.

Chapter Three

"Navigating Higher Education Dreams in the USA Part 1"

Finally, it was time to turn my life-long dream into reality. It was time to start with the necessary preparations beginning with meticulous research, a pursuit fueled by a thirst for knowledge and a desire to ensure the best possible outcome. With countless universities and courses spanning the vast landscape of American education, I compared each institution's offerings and reputation. It was not a choice to be made lightly because it would determine the course of my academic and personal development going forward.

As the decision to immigrate to the United States took center stage, our family gathered for prayers, seeking guidance and reassurance on this life-altering choice. The American Library in Nairobi, Kenya, was a good source of homework on what schools in which state one would like to enroll.

But even hoping for a better future for my family, I faced a significant obstacle: finding the funding needed for this project. The price of international education was high, especially at the prestigious schools I had my heart set on. Along with financial commitment, it required resourcefulness and strategic strategy. Hours were spent looking into grants, scholarships, and other sources of financing that could help with living costs and tuition.

The Black Ostrich

My family's future was heavily on my shoulders as I navigated this financial minefield. My still-developing children served me as a constant source of inspiration and motivation. I was motivated by the conviction that the education and chances I pursued would eventually open the door for them to develop into their greatest potential since their young minds were like fertile ground.

It was a difficult decision to leave my family behind. My young children, who were still under the age of 10, were like anchors in my heart, and the thought of being away from them caused me both fear and resolve. I knew in my heart that this decision was essential for their future and my personal development. The strength I needed to take that first step into the unknown came from the conviction that this sacrifice would bring them chances beyond measure.

My family's support was a crucial source of strength during this time of adjustment. Their support, acceptance, and belief in my choice strengthened my commitment to start this important life journey. My grandfather Jacob, after whom I was named, stood out in particular as a source of knowledge and direction. His blessings, given despite his elderly age, served as evidence of the enduring bond that tied generations together. His steadfast backing of my choice gave me the courage to tackle the difficulties that lay ahead.

The longtime reputation of the United States as a provider of top-notch higher education served as the driving force for my journey there. My curiosity was stoked by the intellectual achievements of the Western world, the variety of viewpoints, and the potential for dialogue with distinguished academics in my field of study. My goals went beyond only receiving a degree; they included challenging my preconceived notions, becoming more knowledgeable, and becoming an open-minded person.

I set out on this journey in pursuit of my aspirations, knowing that it would be filled with a mixture of resolve, uncertainty, and hope.

The route I chose wasn't without its sacrifices. Still, I was confident that these sacrifices would ultimately fulfill dreams that cut across generations and continents.

Chapter Four

"Navigating Higher Education Dreams in the USA Part 2"

There were times when I felt like questioning my choices. I went through periods of doubt about leaving a stable career in teaching, which I had come to love and enjoy. However, individuals up to creating a better tomorrow often encounter such times in their lifetime that put their beliefs to the test, try their resoluteness, and call them into unexplored territory. It is not a choice to be made lightly to leave behind a cherished career, a group of friends, and the daily grind of life, that you are grateful for.

This period in my life's narrative is a turning point where doubt and aspiration collided, where the past crooned in my ear, and the future opened its arms to welcome me.

The practice of teaching had become ingrained in my very being. The classroom transformed into a haven of growth and connection while I nurtured young brains and saw their development. This path's stability was both reassuring and limiting, a duality that frequently tugged at my heart. In the peaceful hours of the evenings, moments of uncertainty would seep in like the shadows of a flickering light. I would often ask myself, *"How could I abandon all I had worked so hard to create?"* *"Was it worth it to give up the sense of accomplishment that came with my teaching career?"* But the heart, that mysterious compass, reminded me that life's greatest chapters often emerge from unexpected beginnings.

For as long as I could remember, I had been rocked to sleep by the siren call of America. I had spent my entire childhood dreaming about going abroad for higher education. I felt a flame within me ignite at the thought of joining America's rich culture and adding to its story. My doubts vanished as I visualized myself navigating the bustling streets of the country jampacked with diverse people and blending into the city's dynamic cultural fabric. It was as if the cosmos had whispered to me, assuring me that my path was meant for much more.

The height of my anxiety, though, was when my visa was granted. A strangely contradictory feeling of excitement and dread filled my veins as the ink on that document dried. It was exciting and terrifying for me to realize that I was about to enter the unknown. The harsh reality that I was now going to face the possibility of being ripped from the roots that had kept me in the country of my origin, where friendships had flourished and familial ties had grown stronger, hit me hard.

Inside of me, the questions raged like a hurricane. *"Could I really leave behind the place where I had smiled, wept, and made a life for myself?" "Would severing the ties that had kept me alive be worth the chase of dreams?"*

A flicker of conviction persisted amid my quest with my mind and inner feelings. It was nothing but an emotional whirlwind. While I was afraid of what the future holds, a part of me was proud of myself for taking this initiative, as in my native Kenya, higher education and the quest for knowledge and development have always been highly valued. The people in my town supported and understood my decision to seek it on foreign soil. Friends and relatives understood the importance of this action because America held a prestigious place in the public mind. A journey to its land was an adventure into a world where potential could grow, dreams could take root, and aspirations could be nurtured. I was able to embrace the road ahead since I knew that my goals were shared by many people and not just mine.

The decision was the result of a balanced combination of culture, curiosity, and heartfelt desire. It served as a transition between the known and the unknown, and the symphonic notes of uncertainty and optimism resonated strongly inside of me. I was going to write a new chapter of my life which would be about courage, vulnerability, and the audacity to steer clear of my fears and follow the beat of my desires.

With all of its intricacies, I realized that this chapter would drastically change the story of my life in ways that were yet unknown as I looked through the pages of my past and the blank pages of my future.

Chapter Five

"Background on Immigrant Communities Part 1"

For immigrants, especially those from East Africa, which includes my native Nairobi, Kenya, the 1990s in the United States were a time of both progress and difficulties. We encountered a landscape full of potential and prejudice as we traveled across oceans in search of possibilities and to pursue our goals. This chapter explores the complicated dynamics of the era, delving into the myths surrounding immigrant favoritism, the difficulties of integration, the barriers to immigration, and the many challenges we faced.

During the time I entered the territory of the US, there were persistent rumors that immigrants were treated better than native-born Americans, but unfortunately, the truth was very different from the perception. Many obstacles stood in the way of immigrants trying to establish themselves. Although some immigrants did succeed quickly, these instances were the exception rather than the rule. The perceived favoritism frequently made our sacrifices and victories difficult to see.

Assimilation was a multi-layered process that differed for each individual. We struggled with trying to fit into American society while still retaining our cultural identities. We faced challenges, including language barriers, disparate social norms, and unfamiliar practices, that we had to overcome. It took tremendous flexibility to strike a balance between our heritage and the demands of our new environment. This complexity was not intended to promote one culture over another but rather to promote respect and understanding among cultures.

Apart from these complexities, Immigration was another intricate procedure that immigrants had to deal with, involving paperwork, waiting, and uncertainty. Work permits, green cards, and visas required navigating complicated bureaucratic procedures. As we awaited immigration clearances, many of us were forced to endure long periods of separation from our families. The process was difficult and required patience, tenacity, and adherence to strict rules; it was not biased against immigration.

For many immigrants, attending college in the United States was a dream come true and a means of achieving success, and there was frequently a high price tag associated with this aspiration. The path to a brighter future was full of substantial obstacles, including the high expense of school, a lack of financial aid for international students, and the scarcity of jobs both during and after their studies. The myth that education inherently ensured success ignored the financial struggles and job insecurity that many of us experienced.

It was a process of awakening and adaptation as we sought our identities. It was extremely demanding to fight to uphold our cultural traditions while adopting American principles. We desired to give back to our chosen country but frequently felt torn between two realities. Our efforts were motivated by our desire to forge connections, add to the cultural diversity, and improve the communities we had just joined.

As I write this manuscript about my personal experiences, it's essential to dispel myths and misconceptions while discussing the experience of immigrants in the 1990s. We, immigrants, didn't have it easy; instead, we faced obstacles head-on in pursuing a better future. Our histories included both successes and setbacks, and our identities were intertwined into the country's rich diversity.

Chapter Six

"Background on Immigrant Communities Part 2"

Empathy serves as a powerful bridge that spans cultures and communities in a world that is growing increasingly interconnected. The importance of empathy, understanding, and social integration within immigrant communities is brought to light by the backdrop of growing interconnectivity. Each of these components works as a catalyst to create a society that is more inclusive and harmonious.

Empathy is the cornerstone of human connection, nurturing an environment where understanding flourishes. Furthermore, embracing and celebrating cultural diversity becomes increasingly important as we recognize the enriching contributions immigrants bring to their new homes. The powerful stories of individuals who have traversed the complex system of immigration contribute to a collective narrative, weaving together shared human experiences and reflections.

Breaking down barriers takes on a pivotal role in fostering the social integration crucial for a cohesive society. Immigrant communities often encounter difficulties as they adjust to their new environments, highlighting the need for measures that foster inclusive environments. This chapter dives into the significance of such initiatives, aiming to promote a strong sense of community for immigrants while valuing the distinctive viewpoints they contribute to the social mosaic.

This chapter sheds light on the significant events that unfolded during the 1990s and beyond, illuminating a transformative era marked by notable shifts in the United States.

During the 1990s, several notable events within the US immigration system had significant implications for Black Americans:

(A)Immigration Act of 1990: The Immigration Act of 1990 brought about changes to the US immigration system, including an increase in the number of available visas and the establishment of the Diversity Visa program. While not exclusively aimed at Black immigrants, these changes provided new avenues for immigrants from underrepresented countries, including those in Africa and the Caribbean.

(B) Amendments to the Immigration and Nationality **Act:** The Immigration Act of 1990 also introduced changes to the preference system, which impacted family-based immigration. This could have affected Black Americans seeking to reunite with family members abroad.

(C) Haitian Refugee Crisis: The 1990s saw a significant

number of Haitian refugees attempting to seek asylum in the United States due to political instability in Haiti. This led to debates and legal challenges over immigration policies and the treatment of Haitian immigrants.

(D) Temporary Protected Status (TPS): Some Black immigrants from countries facing conflict or natural disasters were granted Temporary Protected Status during the 1990s, allowing them to stay and work in the US temporarily. This impacted individuals from countries like Liberia and Somalia.

(E) 1996 Immigration Laws: The Illegal Immigration Reform and Immigrant Responsibility Act of 1996 introduced changes to immigration policies. While these changes affected immigrants overall, they could have specific implications for Black immigrants in terms of deportation policies and access to certain benefits.

(F) Debates on Affirmative Action: Affirmative action policies, while not exclusive to immigration, were widely discussed during the 1990s. These discussions could impact Black immigrants' access to education and employment opportunities.

(G) Advocacy and Community Initiatives: Throughout the 1990s, advocacy groups and community organizations focused on immigration rights, including those that had a direct impact on Black immigrants. These efforts aimed to address issues such as deportation, legal status, and equitable treatment.

It's crucial to remember that while these incidents affected the immigration landscape in the 1990s, they were only a small element of a larger system of immigration laws that impacted individuals from all backgrounds. The experiences of Black immigrants during this era were shaped by a combination of these events and their unique circumstances.

Chapter Seven

"Applying for the American Student Visa"

The American Student Visa application process was truly scary. Long application forms had to be filled out, documents had to be gathered into a single bundle, and then they had to be submitted for visa approval.

As much as I was thrilled to embark on this journey, the decision to pursue higher education in the US held both promise and uncertainty. I had to go through a complex web of requirements and difficulties when I started the process of applying for a student visa, which taught me the value of planning and patience.

Contrary to what I had imagined, obtaining an American Student Visa turned out to be a difficult process that required close attention to detail and perseverance to get things done. I applied to study auto mechanics at Chattahoochee Technical Community College in Marietta, based on which I applied for my Student Visa.

Furthermore, the American Student Visa application process revealed a shocking maze of paperwork and criteria that had to be fulfilled in order to obtain the visa. The initial challenge was overcoming the complexities of filling out forms, acquiring necessary paperwork, and navigating the bureaucracy of the visa application procedure. As a prospective student, I had to deal with the challenges of demonstrating my desire to study, having the money to pay for my education and living expenses, and meeting the strict visa requirements.

But that's not all. The challenges that arose during this procedure, though, went beyond simple bureaucratic issues and affected every aspect of the journey. The uncertainty of approval and the concern over meeting the required financial responsibilities loomed overhead. The pressure of meeting my family's expectations and the strain on my finances caused additional difficulties that put my determination and drive to the test, yet I kept going. While there were moments when it felt like a never-ending procedure, I kept pushing myself to get through this.

As I look back to those days, I remember developing effective plans and strategies to overcome these difficulties and lighten the burden that was wearing my shoulders down. With the help of research, I dug deeply into understanding the complex procedures and criteria. I reached out to individuals in the same boat to better understand how to go about the visa application process. Making a strong personal statement emerged as a critical component that allowed me to express my goals and reasons in detail.

I think it's difficult to effectively prepare for such a huge life transition. However, once you streamline your tasks, things will start to come into shape, and you will begin to see a light at the end of the tunnel. Naturally, there are typical procedures that must be followed, such as giving up immediate home belongings, getting authorization to travel, and applying for visas.

During this journey, I came to understand the critical significance of making well-informed decisions. My own experience emphasizes how important it is to fully understand the landscape, legal system, and cultural specifics of the host nation where you are going to pursue your higher education.

This bumpy phase of my life has taught me that while the charm of new beginnings can be captivating, it is important not to lose focus on the ultimate goal, conduct careful research, and know about the dos and don'ts of life in the United States.

Indeed, with resilience and hard work, you can make the

impossible possible.

Chapter Eight

"How it All Began Migration Without Family Part 1"

March 16, 1996,

(Just a week before my grand journey to the US)

The golden ticket—my visa—finally came after months of hard work and the constant support of my family. I can vividly recall the day when the embassy called to ask me to pick up my passport. It was supposed to be a day of celebration, but there was also a sense of sorrow because this achievement meant saying goodbye to my wife and our two little champions.

My brother Kenneth, a longtime resident of the US, was extremely helpful during the preparations, assisting me through the confusing visa application procedure and showing me the way forward. However, when I began this unfamiliar path, I found myself fending off uncertainty like a tightrope dancer in a storm.

Finding work immediately after arriving in America was my top priority because it would serve as the foundation for my journey toward independence. The days before leaving were a whirlwind of tearful goodbyes to friends and relatives, with each hug becoming a priceless memory from which I could take courage.

The Black Ostrich

As the departure date approached, an upsurge of emotions and a storm of worry raged inside me. However, my wife's constant presence helped me get through this tough phase, guiding me through the storm. Her uplifting comments were all I needed the most at that time.

My wife and I had a soul-baring talk the night before my flight after putting our children to bed. With each syllable, we made promises of resiliency and of facing separation head-on into our hearts. I promised her that despite the distance, my commitment would not change. I vowed to fill the gap between us, whether it required a sympathetic ear or financial support.

Finally, the day of departure had come. I put on my best clothes, nestling my paperwork safely and holding my passport in one hand. I gave my family members a passionate kiss on the cheeks, soaking up their warmth and love. My parents' blessings poured down on me, giving me courage like a kind gift. At that very moment, I felt an eruption of emotions as I stepped through the front door of my house, fusing exhilaration and nervousness into a strong brew.

A Nissan Sunny cab was waiting for me outside to take me to the airport. The trip to the airport seemed both endless and brief, serving as a prologue to the upcoming tremendous journey.

After clearing the security and check-in, I sought comfort in a nook of the airport lounge, where I plunged into a sea of thought amidst the activity of other travelers. As the anticipation-woven patterns of ideas unfolded, doubts and hopes danced in a delicate waltz. The excitement of what lay ahead was mixed with the sadness of leaving behind my family. One thing became clear amid this emotional whirlwind: My family was my compass and my reason for existing. They were my motivation to settle and thrive in the unknown land I was going to travel.

Yet time seemed to slip through my fingers like sand as my mind traveled inward. I was startled out of my trance by the announcement of boarding. I quickly joined the stream of travelers who were making their way to the plane.

The aircraft's slow climb felt like my own ascent into a new life, and the cabin greeted me with open arms as the engines roared to life. I curled up in my seat and gave in to sleep, the steady hum of the engines soothing me.

Hours passed quickly, and when I finally woke up, I had the bizarre realization that we were only a short distance away from where I was going. My heart beat quickly as excitement swept through me as the plane descended. Although the journey had been lengthy, the end was in sight, and my life was about to change.

The wheels gently bounced back into contact with the ground. Touchdown! Holding onto my armrest, I heard the plane's wheels grind against the tarmac. Rather than being frightened by the turbulence, my heart was racing since I had just started a brand-new chapter in my life. I felt a wave of anticipation, tiredness, and a tinge of anxiety as the plane drew to a stop. I pulled off my seatbelt, adjusted my collar, and inhaled deeply.

We were welcomed to the country and thanked for picking their airline as the captain's voice chimed over the loudspeaker. There was no turning back now, I reasoned. I gathered my belongings, including my always-present passport, and I joined the queue of eager passengers waiting to get off the ship.

I arrived at a busy international airport's chaos as soon as I stepped off the plane. Although there were clear signs pointing me in the direction of immigration, the sheer number of people was a little daunting. I made an effort to maintain my composure by reminding myself that this wouldn't take long, hopefully.

I shuffled through my file as I drew nearer the immigration desk to make sure I had all the necessary paperwork. While I waited, I watched the officers at work; each expressionless face resembled a spy movie figure. When I approached the desk, a stern-looking officer inquired about my reason for visiting, my expected stay time, and my intended lodging. He stamped my passport and returned it after being satisfied with my responses.

I stepped away from the counter, believing that the immigration process had gone flawlessly. However, just as I was about to sigh with relief, a loud voice said, "Sir, would you mind moving this way?" My heart performed a backflip, and I suddenly believed that I had unintentionally packed either a stowaway squirrel or a prohibited fruit.

As I followed a stern-looking officer into a small room, my palms began to sweat. A few travelers were seated there, their faces varying from mild irritation to outright terror. I sat down and looked nervously over at the man seated next to me. I muttered to myself, "Great, the first turn in my great adventure!"

An officer finally called my name after what seemed like an eternity. I followed him to another counter while my legs were slightly shaky as I got to my feet. He took my passport, looked at me, then turned his attention back to it. I could feel the minutes passing like seconds.

Then, though, the most shocking event took place. Your convincing power is unparalleled, for sure, the officer said as he glanced up from my passport. I blinked in shock, unsure of how to react. "*I reviewed your immigration application,*" he said, "*and your narrative is extremely interesting. Right, you're here to please your family.*"

Still unsure of where this was leading, I nodded.

"*Well, it seems like you've got yourself into big trouble,*" he remarked, cracking a smile. "*Your luggage apparently didn't make it on this trip owing to a mix-up. You shouldn't worry, though; we've found it, and we'll bring it to your location soon.*"

I laughed, a laugh that was both relieved and sincere. *Who would have imagined that my first surprise in this new country would be a mistake with my luggage?* I murmured to myself.

I couldn't help but laugh as I walked out of the airport at the comedy of the circumstance. Although I had prepared myself for the challenges of a new life, my worst adversary ended up being a lost suitcase. I knew that even in the face of unpredictable storms, a little humor might go a long way in keeping my spirits high, so I called a taxi and made my way to the city.

Chapter Nine

"How it All Began Migration Without Family Part 2"

As soon as I set foot on the ground of beautiful South Carolina, known for its white sand beaches, warm temperatures, parks and festivals, etc, I immediately called a cab. I sat in the backseat with my heart racing, feeling a pang of fatigue due to the hours-long flight. However, a surge of excitement rushed through my veins as I peeked outside the window, observing each mile, bringing me one step closer to the next chapter of my life.

The cab went through streets that were unfamiliar to me yet held the promise of a new beginning, guided by the address I clutched in my fingers. The car finally came to a stop, and I looked out at the house - It was our family friend's home that would serve as my temporary accommodation—a place created out of a generous spirit.

My parents' dearest friend opened the door for me to realize my dream of studying at Greenville Technical College, SC. If it wasn't for them, I wouldn't be able to come to this foreign land as I had no accommodation and means of transportation. They offered me guidance throughout, and there was never a dull moment with them where I would feel like an outsider.

I took a deep breath as I took my first step to the main door. The door slid wide to reveal a room brimming with affection and memories. The house exuded the comforting embrace of connection and affection. The walls seemed to be telling stories from bygone eras while conversations within carried the echoes of long-gone laughter.

South Carolina, with its picturesque towns and rich scenery, served as my canvas for development. A harmonious fusion of the ancient and new could be heard in the sounds of the frantic city life mingling with the rustling of leaves. I couldn't help but be in awe of the experiences I was creating as I walked through the maze of streets and buildings each day.

Fast forward to college life at Greenville Technical institute. My college life was like something I had always dreamt of. Every classroom and library session had left traces of people who had gone before me. The campus seemed to ooze progress and community, which was a tribute to the ideals I upheld.

Contrary to what I had imagined, I found myself surrounded by classmates, as well as got a grip on the courses and lectures, within a span of a few weeks. I made some genuine friends during my college life with whom I shared my career and life goals. Together, we lifted each other up to help each of us achieve our goals.

I wanted to join the college partly because the program was sponsored by the automotive behemoths Ford, GM, and Chrysler, offering me the ability to forge my own path. General Motors had already ventured into Kenya, and a school tour one day nailed my decision to join Greenville Technical College.

As I became more involved in academic life, I found a world that was far more thrilling than I could have ever imagined. Classes started to become more than just lectures; they were explorations guided by passionate teachers who stoked my interest in learning.

My friends not only helped me find my way around the large campus of the institution, but also exposed me to the lively local culture. Our hangouts turned into excursions that took us to other parts of South Carolina. Weekends weren't just rest days; they were also filled with plans for memorable adventures that would go down in my scrapbook of experiences.

However, to earn this life, I had to work full-time jobs so that I could pay for my expenses. Although my brother, Kenneth, offered financial assistance, I wanted to be on my own. The pride of making my own money gave me a sense of empowerment that helped me get through the difficulties ahead of me. I, therefore, had to work two full-time jobs in addition to my engineering studies to make ends meet.

Time moved quickly, and I gained more stability each day. Just like that, a year passed characterized by tenacity, and a few well-earned achievements. Luckily, by then, I had saved enough funds to offer a comfortable life to my family in the US.

Finally, it was time to fulfill the promise I made to my wife, which was to reunite with them—my wife and children—in this land of opportunities.

While I had imagined a different journey for myself, a smooth one, destiny, ever the unpredictable writer, had planned a turn that would contradict my story. A sudden storm was forming, one that would make history in the American culture.

I was unaware that the following circumstances would throw me into a struggle for survival and put my fortitude to the test. The threat of danger lurked in the distance, serving as a reminder that success frequently comes with unexpected difficulties. I stood firm in the road, ready to put up the fight of a lifetime while my family's destiny hung in the balance.

Soon, the stark reality that awaited immigrants in the United States, especially those of black origin, was about to emerge. Beyond the secured walls of university life, a completely different world existed, unknown to me.

Chapter Ten

"Dreams and Dilemmas Studying Abroad"

The day had finally come, a day I had eagerly anticipated ever since I first set foot in the United States. It was the day my family was due to arrive. That was the day my family was supposed to get here. I'd worked nonstop for a year, and now I had found them a safe place in this new world of possibility. There was a buzz of excitement in the airport terminal as I waited for them to arrive.

I started crying as soon as I saw them enter through the arrival gate. I hurried to give them a hug as my heart swelled with gratitude and joy. I had never felt an embrace as warm and sincere as the one I had with my wife and kids. That day, being reunited with my family, was undoubtedly the best event of my life.

The days that followed were a blur of transitions and fresh starts. My kids needed to get back into school, so we started looking for schools right away. Our children, who had already faced their share of hardships, encountered a different challenge in their new American schools: bullying. Unlike me, my children were being picked out because of their racial differences. Maybe it was because I had always been the one to confront bullies and done well in college back home.

As I helped my kids adjust to their new schools, I kept working in several positions in the hospitality sector. For short stints, I also worked as an auto mechanic and a lawnmower repair technician. But while I was going to college, I worked full-time as a "Floor Technician," which is just a fancy way of pronouncing "janitor." Although it was a humble experience, I had to do it in order to provide for my family and pay the bills.

We were definitely experiencing culture shock, as is typical for many recent immigrants. Thankfully, we had previously grasped English, making the transition easier. We did, however, encounter our fair share of difficulties. Racism showed up in both the colleges I attended and my place of employment. As an immigrant, I wasn't always aware of the dog whistles and subliminal signs of racism at first, but I eventually developed a greater awareness of the prejudice that was present but went unnoticed.

Most of the discrimination I experienced was overt, and it came from both African Americans and my white coworkers. Some African Americans, surprisingly, confronted me upfront because of the false belief that immigrants received preferential treatment. I later came to understand this phenomenon as a form of "divide and rule," a strategy that pits different racial and ethnic groups against one another. Conversely, I couldn't help but observe that when African Americans came to our nation, they were frequently greeted with a great deal of respect and loyalty. Before moving to the US, I had personally welcomed a large number of African-American guests, most of whom were American-born friends of my parents.

Despite these difficulties, our kids achieved academic success yet again. As they adjusted to their new surroundings, their perseverance and determination were evident. I had to work several odd jobs to make ends meet while constantly aiming to give my family the finest living possible in our new house.

The start of this new life was indeed difficult. However, with my family by my side, it never felt challenging. My wife was my constant support throughout this tough phase. We knew that the road ahead would be marked by unpredictable challenges. But as a family, we were determined to persevere, to overcome the racism and adversity that came our way, and to build a better future in this country.

Chapter Eleven

"FY 1998 Diversity Visa Lottery Program"

Life bestows countless opportunities but only to those looking for them. Those who strive for them, spot them right on and make the most of them. Something like this happened to me back in the year 1998 when I got the chance to get permanent residence in the US to secure my family's future.

My journey to secure permanent residency in the United States began with a piece of paper, a mere lottery ticket, and a profound stroke of luck.

It was 1998 when my fate offered me a seemingly unbelievable opportunity - The Diversity Visa (DV) lottery program - My best chance to obtain a green card and finally open the door to world-class education and endless possibilities.

The Diversity Visa lottery, also known as the Green Card lottery, was established in 1990 as part of the Immigration Act. Its primary aim was to foster diversity among immigrants by granting visas to individuals from countries with historically low immigration rates to the United States. Countries like Kenya, which were underrepresented in the federal population, became eligible for this program.

The program, which has been in effect since 1990, is run like a lottery, said Charles Kuck, a Buckhead attorney proficient in immigration law.

"It's open to people with either a high school diploma or two years of work experience in a job that requires experience in that field. You send in a piece of paper with your name, picture, and fingerprint signature, and a computer randomly picks winners," he said.

The idea was straightforward but revolutionary. Like myself, applicants from qualified nations might enter the lottery by sending in a piece of paper containing our name, picture, fingerprints, and signature in addition to our basic biographical data. After that, a computer program would choose the lucky winners at random to obtain one of the most sought-after Diversity Visas. These visas, which offered the possibility of permanent residency and, eventually, the opportunity to become citizens of the United States, were the keys to a new life in the country.

There was intense rivalry each year, with hundreds of thousands of candidates competing for about 55,000 visas globally. Although the odds were overwhelming, the rewards were priceless for those who prevailed, like myself.

It was Feb 2, 1998, when I took the leap of faith and finally turned in all my paperwork for the Diversity Visa lottery seven months in advance, along with the required fee, with hope and confidence in my heart. The wait was agonizing and laden with uncertainty and expectation. Yet, all my family and I could do was speculate about what the future might bring.

Then, one fateful day, the letter arrived with news that would forever alter our lives. Among the lucky few who would be granted a Diversity Visa was me. It was a moment of overwhelming joy when I realized my dreams were no longer just fantasies. I still remember my words when I received the notice that I had won the lottery, I was like, *"No.. it can't be true. Is this really happening, or am I dreaming?"* It was a big shock. It was incredible.

However, the journey was far from ending. The DV lottery program had deadlines and a rigid set of guidelines. Being chosen was not sufficient; I also needed to submit my application on time and have it accepted for the fiscal year that I applied. Any unanticipated issues, administrative backlogs, or delays could destroy the chance I had worked so hard to obtain.

I was granted a chance by the Diversity Visa lottery, but it also came with obligations and a sense of urgency. I was now on a quest to successfully go through the convoluted immigration procedure, making sure that all requirements were satisfied, all paperwork was filed, and all obstacles were overcome.

Before setting out on this life-changing adventure, I couldn't help but think back on the amazing good fortune that had brought me this far. The winning of the Diversity Visa lottery was evidence of the American dream, which had inspired optimism in my heart and was now attainable. I was prepared to face whatever comes my way. I was prepared to fight my challenges head-on to avail myself of this opportunity no matter what.

Chapter Twelve

"Challenges with Immigration Services"

You can never tell what one is going through until you step into their shoes. Never had I ever realized how flawed US immigration was until I saw it with my own eyes. That time was the beginning of my darker years. Those were the years I struggled to keep the justice system alive. I fought for myself and so many others like me.

So, back to the time when I won the Diversity Lottery program. I did everything required of me. In fact, I submitted all the required documents seven months before the deadline, Sept 30, 1998.

After submission, I took a sigh of relief, thinking that was all I had to do. However, as the months went by, I began to feel anxious as there was no word from the government. As much as I wanted to investigate what was going wrong with my case, my hands were tied by the standard warning issued by the immigration services. The federal immigration agency sent a letter to applicants that said, in part, *"Please DO NOT make inquiries as to the status of your case, as it will result in further delay."* I followed the instructions and did not write or call to check on my application.

The feeling of anxiousness was now turning into distress. Somewhere in my heart, I knew things were not going well. The months-long wait was now stretching into years. Luckily, I was not solely relying on my lottery visa and kept renewing my work visa. All the while, I had been expecting that my visa application would be reviewed.

Things went on like this until 2001, when we were shocked to the core by an email that my wife, Doin Kibaara, received, stating that she needed to obtain a visa in order to remain in the country. At that very moment, we realized that something had gone very wrong because my family had been included in the paperwork I submitted as a lottery winner. Their status was directly connected to mine. It was devastating. I just couldn't believe it. Those were my exact words. We were in their correspondence throughout, and they knew I had turned in all the required paperwork on time.

Apparently, seven months wasn't enough time for an overworked immigration office to process my application. Upon contacting them, they told me that they couldn't find my application file. What was even worse was despite being at fault, the government was intent on sending me and my family back to Kenya.

The immigration agency did not process that application before the deadline. As a result, the US Immigration and Naturalization Service Later told me that my legal standing to remain in the United States expired at midnight on Sept. 30, 1998, the last day of the federal budget year.

The agency reasoned that the people who win the "diversity lottery" are eligible for a visa only in the same budget year in which they are chosen. If applicants don't receive a visa that year, they face expulsion even if they applied in plenty of time.

Immigration officials, however, failed to process my paperwork before the deadline, and I was l left with no choice but to resort to the courts to seek justice and prevent the government from sending us back.

It was the beginning of a decade long battle that I did not only fight for myself but for the entire immigrant community.

Charles

An oversight by U.S. immigration officials has aspiring pastor from Kenya caught in a bureaucratic ...

Photos by ANDY SHARP / Staff

Charles Nyaga wants to continue enjoying the life he has built for himself in the U.S., but the native Kenyan faces possible expulsion because of a bureaucratic misstep. He applied for a visa as he was supposed to, but officials failed to process it on time.

No man's land

Chapter Thirteen

"Flawed System Denied Asylum and More"

Amidst the challenging times of immigration bureaucracy enveloped in the darkness of isolation, I was convinced that my struggles were unique. I used to question my fate and why only I must bear the weight of these immigration woes alone while others enjoy their lives in this land of opportunities with no fear of deportation or facing immigration issues. Little did I know that a family from Palestine had been struggling with a battle like mine for over a decade.

A small Palestinian family comprising six family members, Bassam Garadah, his wife Maha Dakar, and their four daughters, all US-born, were living with the fear of deportation due to the courtesy of the broken immigration system of the United States.

The Garadah family story is about how the American dream turned into an immigration nightmare. In 1998, Bassam Garadah and his wife, Maha Dakar, both Palestinians, applied for political asylum in the USA. In the ensuing nine years, the couple made a good life, raising four daughters born in America, all younger than 10. After a decade-long process of court hearings and appeals, the 6th Circuit Court of Appeals came back with a final decision on their asylum petition: denied. The family was left scrambling about what to do next.

The nation's immigration debate has been largely about the 12 million illegal immigrants in this country. But little attention has been paid to law-abiding immigrants whose families have suffered long delays and errors because of backlogs at the U.S. Citizenship and Immigration Services (USCIS) and FBI.

So, Maha Dakar was being threatened with deportation, meaning the family would likely be split apart. Several years ago, the couple tried to improve their odds by also applying for residency through their immediate relatives in the USA. But their applications would take at least five years - well beyond Maha's deportation deadline. Their situation became more complicated by the family's background. Maha is a Jordanian citizen of Palestinian descent. She would be deported to Jordan. Bassam, who carried only Egyptian travel documents, had been refused entry to both Egypt and Jordan. The couple lived in Bulgaria and Kuwait before immigrating to the USA. However, Kuwait would not allow the entire family to return because Palestinians do not have citizenship rights. (In fact, the judge, in rejecting their asylum request, the judge mistakenly ruled that they could return to Kuwait without facing persecution.)

Aside from reflecting the poor state of U.S. immigration services, the Garadah story also highlights how stateless and displaced Palestinian refugees, who number more than 4 million, are often mistreated in host countries. The refugees often are treated as second-class citizens. For those reasons and others, the Garadah family felt privileged to live in America.

On July 30. Rep. Steve Chabot, R-Ohio, introduced a bill that allowed Maha to remain in the US while her immigration application was being considered. Chabot has been strongly opposed to illegal immigration, but he has said that Garadah family members entered the country legally. They had broken no laws and should be allowed to stay in, given that their daughters are US citizens. After Chabot's bill was introduced, USCIS decided not to enforce Maha's deportation until March 2009. Still, such bills are usually symbolic and have rarely passed, and when they do, only an individual or family is helped.

Delayed applications can make the daily lives of these immigrants quite difficult.

Charles

The Garadah family has not traveled outside the USA in the past 10 years out of fear of being refused re-entry. Maha and Bassam also must apply for a work permit every year, making it difficult to hold down a job because their authorization papers often arrive months late, or sometimes not at all. Applicants often face difficulties obtaining driver's licenses, opening bank accounts, and establishing a credit history to buy a home or a car.

The fact that immigrants are willing to wait out the seemingly interminable immigration process shows the value that they place on living in the USA. Yet how does the nation reward them for trying the legal path? It allows their applications to become entangled in a bureaucracy that will ultimately fail many of them.

Chapter Fourteen

"The Elusive Green Card Navigating Immigration Complexities"

I knew I had to fight with everything I had as I stood on the edge of losing the life I had created in the United States. It was obvious that I had been let down by the immigration system, and it was my responsibility to pursue justice using the appropriate legal channels. My family's future was in jeopardy, and I couldn't handle the idea of being apart from them.

I went to an immigration lawyer for advice, a desperation-driven resolve burning in my heart. We started a legal struggle together that would test my endurance, fortitude, and confidence in the American judicial system.

The first step was to file a lawsuit against the INS for their failure to process my visa application in a timely manner. It was a daunting task, taking on a bureaucratic behemoth that seemed indifferent to the lives it was affecting. But I couldn't back down, not when the well-being of my family was at stake.

Finally, in 2001, I sued the INS for the disruption they had caused. The legal process was complex and time-consuming. We meticulously gathered evidence, documented every communication with immigration officials, and prepared a compelling case to present in court. It was a painstaking process, and there were moments when doubt and frustration threatened to consume me.

But I drew strength from the support of my family, who stood by my side patiently. My wife, Doin, was my biggest source of strength, her energy matching my own. Being together, we managed to set aside our uncertainties with a strong commitment and determination so that we can provide a better life to our children.

As the legal battle raged on, I couldn't help but reflect on the irony of my situation. I had come to the United States with dreams of a better life, only to find myself entangled in a bureaucratic nightmare. Yet, I clung to the belief that justice would prevail, that the very system I was challenging would ultimately do right by us.

Months turned into years, and our case slowly wound its way through the courts. The emotional toll was immense, but I knew I had to stay the course. I thought of all the others like me who had fallen victim to a system that seemed broken beyond repair. I was fighting not just for my family but for every immigrant who had faced injustice.

Finally, after what felt like an eternity, a ray of hope appeared as a US District Court judge in Atlanta ordered authorities to grant me a visa. The courts began to recognize the gravity of our situation and the injustice we had endured. The legal battle was far from over, but it seemed that the wheels of justice were finally turning in our favor.

"The government admits the INS Atlanta district office did not follow its own policy and procedures," the judge wrote. The immigration service, *"offers no explanation for this failure to act, aside from suggesting that INS has more work that it can handle, which is not a very satisfying explanation."*

She ordered INS, which had been broken up into three agencies, to process my visa application as if the 1998 deadline had not passed.

However, in 2002, the 11th US Circuit Court of Appeals in Atlanta ruled that immigration authorities lacked grounds to grant me a visa, stating that I became ineligible for a visa at midnight Sept 30, 1998, even though 35,000 of the 55,000 visas set aside in that year's

Diversity lottery were never claimed. The US Supreme Court declined three months ago to hear my case.

LAW OFFICES
WHELCHEL & DUNLAP, LLP

WILLIAM A. BAGWELL
WILLIAM L. ROGERS, JR.
JOHN A. GRAM
EDGAR B. DUNLAP, II
THOMAS M. COLE
MADELINE S. WIRT
EMILY C. BAGWELL
BETHANY A. SAULS

405 WASHINGTON STREET, N.E.
P.O. BOX ONE
GAINESVILLE, GEORGIA 30503

SUCCESSOR TO
SAMUEL C. DUNLAP (1848-1920)
DUNLAP & DUNLAP
WHELCHEL, DUNLAP & GIGNILLIAT
EDGAR B. DUNLAP (1892-1955)
WILLIAM P. WHELCHEL (1895-1975)

OF COUNSEL
JAMES A. DUNLAP

TELEPHONE (770) 532-7211
FAX (770) 532-7361

May 1, 2002

VIA REGULAR MAIL

Charles Nyaga
5216 Glendora Court
Powder Springs, GA 30127

Dear Charles:

As we have discussed, the U.S. Supreme Court has denied our request to hear your case. Enclosed is the written notification. I also enclose several copies of the Petition we filed with the Supreme Court, as well as, a copy of our latest bill.

Sincerely,

WHELCHEL & DUNLAP, LLP

Madeline

Madeline S. Wirt

Now, my only salvation would be if a US legislator sponsors a bill in Congress that addresses the immigration snafu. Charles Kuck, who had been handling my case pro bono, said introducing such a bill would suspend the deportation process while Congress is in session.

MDJ Feb 9,2004

Immigration snafu may force family out of U.S.

Hopes hinge on Chambliss' bill proposal

By Joan Durbin
Marietta Daily Journal Staff Writer

POWDER SPRINGS — Time is running out for Charles Nyaga. Because of a mistake in his immigration paperwork, he and his family may soon be forced to leave the country they have called home for the past eight years.

By all accounts, Nyaga, a 46-year-old Kenyan national, has built a productive, satisfying life in America. He is two years away from a divinity degree, a career change he chose after the 2002 death of his father, a pastor.

His studies are interspersed with his job as concierge at the Marietta Conference Center and Resort, where his employer sings Nyaga's praise. "His duties are always done well, and he finds many other ways of helping guests," MCC General Manager Jim Keller said. "What makes him a

particularly favorite target of positive comment cards is the class and style he directs to each person who enters our doors. Many people wear a smile all day, but Charles has a smile that is warm, comforting and sincere."

Nyaga recently received the "Superstar" award from Remington Hospitality, MCC's management company, an award given to associates who are leaders in guest services, Keller said.

Sundays, Nyaga can be found at Marietta's Southminster Presbyterian Church. He's an elder there, a favorite of the congregation, who they say contributes significantly to the spiritual life and well-being of the church.

Jan Boehm, a church member and a friend of Nyaga's since 1996, said he is "just a wonderful human being, so decent and forthright.

"He's highly motivated to be a good husband, father, church mem-

ber and citizen," she said.

Unless a miracle happens, however, Nyaga's life is about to undergo drastic change.

On Feb. 20, Nyaga must report for

Charles Nyaga of Powder Springs looks over his immigration paperwork. Nyaga is fighting to remain in the country, but a mistake by the immigration and Naturalization Services may force him and his family to leave the country.

Staff photo by Damien A. Guzman

a court hearing that could lead to his deportation.

Nyaga has been in the United

See Family, Page 5A

Georgia Sen. Saxby Chambliss (R. Moultrie) said he would sponsor the legislation, but nothing had happened, Kuck said. Massive casework overloads at immigration services prevent my paperwork from being processed on time, said my lawyer, Charles Kuck of Atlanta.

"Like (Nyaga), there are many good people trying to do what it takes but get burned by the system," said Kuck. He said it should have taken less than a year for me to receive my green card.

The Black Ostrich

In March 2004, I was notified that a federal immigration judge denied my request to apply for an adjustment to my immigration status and ordered me to leave the country within 60 days. The order was upheld by the Board of Immigration Appeals.

There were many people who had the same kind of problem like mine. Congress at that time was trying to investigate what the problems were.

Even though I turned in the required application and fees seven months before the deadline, I failed to understand why authorities seemed so intent on denying me a visa that all sides agreed I was once entitled to receive.

In a system like this, one person like me doesn't matter, but that one person is me.

The most frustrating thing is that despite playing by the government rules, I became the victim due to their incompetency.

The Rev. W. ROBERT FLOYD, ThM., D.Min.
Licensed Professional Counselor ◇ Licensed Marriage & Family Therapist
11424 Rolling Brook Road ◇ Chester, Virginia 23831
(804) 748-4859 ◇ wrfloyd@earthlink.net

November 17, 2005

The Honorable J. Randy Forbes
307 Cannon House Office Building
Washington, DC 20515

Dear Randy:

Thank you for your letter of November 9, 2005, in response to my letter of August 31. It gives us grateful confidence in your representation of us when you respond to our heartfelt requests.

I appreciate and heartily agree with your statement of your strong stand on control of illegal immigration. Unfortunately, however, you did not respond to the primary plea of my letter – desperately needed help for Mr. Charles Nyaga and all the other law-abiding legal immigrants who came into this country via the immigration "Lottery" and who are moral, hard-working, intelligent people who will be a great asset to America. These fine people have been abused by the I.N.S. staff with threats of deportation simply because staff workers did not get around to processing applications, even though Mr. Nyaga submitted his application **SEVEN MONTHS** prior to the stipulated deadline!!!

Please re-read my enclosed letter of August 31 and take action on my request for redress of this despicable situation. I shall look forward to your speedy reply, hoping that this will become a priority for your zealous and expeditious action.

Sincerely in faith,

W. Robert Floyd, Th.M.,D.Min.

Chapter Fifteen

"Living With the Fear of Deportation"

Amidst the chaos, I found a home away from home at Southminster Presbyterian Church, where I teach Sunday school, preach occasionally, and have helped to revitalize the youth program. The church has been a source of strength for me during my immigration ordeal.

By all accounts, over the course of those ten years, I had built a productive, satisfying life in America. I was two years away from a divinity degree, a career change I chose after the 2002 death of his father, a pastor.

My studies are interspersed with my job as concierge at the Marietta Conference Center and Resort, where my employer sings my praise.

"His duties are always done well, and he finds many other ways of helping guests," MCC General Manager Jim Keller said. *"What makes him a particularly favorite target of positive comment cards is the class and style he directs to each person who enters our doors. Many people wear a smile all day, but Charles has a smile that is warm, comforting, and sincere."*

"Nyaga recently received the 'Superstar' award from Remington Hospitality, MCC's management company, an award given to

associates who are leaders in guest services," Keller added.

"S*undays, Nyaga can be found at Marietta's Southminster Presbyterian Church. He's an elder there, a favorite of the congregation, who they say contributes significantly to the spiritual life and well-being of the church.*"

Jan Boehm, a church member and a friend of mine since 1996, said he is *"just a wonderful human being, so decent and forthright in helping the guests."*

"He's highly motivated to be a good husband, father, church member, and citizen," she said.

Later, a spokeswoman for Chambliss said the senator wants to tweak the law to help a handful of foreign nationals in my situation-people who win a rare shot at legal status through a government diversity lottery but face expulsion because authorities don't review their applications in time. Chambliss could introduce a bill in the next few weeks, said Angie Lundberg, the spokeswoman.

Joe Jacquot, who handles immigration issues for Chambliss, said he knows of a dozen people nationwide in similar straits. He said Chambliss' bill would affect people who participated in past diverse lotteries and that the Department of Homeland Security plans to change regulations to prevent a repeat of what happened to us.

"We are well aware of his situation. We're going to solve it for him," Jacquot said.

Meanwhile, I kept my faith strong because that's the only thing you can do during such calamitic times.

In February 2004, when he was chairman of the Senate immigration subcommittee, Chambliss submitted a bill that would have allowed officials to reconsider some visa applications like mine that had expired due to government inaction. Chambliss' bill bought us some time, until a month later, when Atlanta Immigration Judge William A. Cassidy ordered me to leave the country within two months.

That same year, I traveled to Washington, D.C., and appeared before a Congressional subcommittee investigating possible corruption in the diversity visa program. Sen. Saxby Chambliss (R-Moultrie) had been working to get legislation passed to help me and other immigration cases like me. The legislation would have given the Department of Homeland Security a chance to reopen Diversity Visa lottery cases from previous fiscal years to complete processing. The bill ultimately failed, but Chambliss' work was recognized and appreciated.

Chambliss tried again the following year, attaching his proposal to an emergency Iraq war supplemental appropriations bill. Chambliss also tried a couple of so-called private bills designed to help only me in 2005 and 2007, but they didn't get out of committee.

On Feb. 20, I was told by my attorney that I must report for a court hearing that could lead to my deportation.

Things were nowhere even close to getting resolved. I remember those darkest days when I had just put my head to the pillow as the dreaded knock came at the door of my Powder Springs home. It was around 6 o'clock when I came home weary from working all night at my cleaning job, looked out on my front porch, and saw three Immigration and Customs Enforcement agents standing before me.

They bore handcuffs. "I was praying," "What else can you do?"

The agents cuffed me and my wife and took us downtown. Things could not have seemed bleaker or more unfair.

Fortunately, I was in custody only for one day. "We were able to get him released right away with Senator Chambliss' intervention," Kuck said.

A bureaucratic mistake by the former INS agency in 1998 had stymied my family's proper and initially successful efforts to become legal permanent US residents and, someday, we hoped, American citizens.

Now, with the threat of deportation looming every minute, we may finally get a break. For ten years, my wife and two children had waited and worried, hoping to get the green cards that would grant them permanent legal residence in the United States before immigration officials decided to deport them.

We were devastated, but we were not defeated. We were stripped of everything, but we were not alone. We knew that we would get through this with the help of those who cared about us. We had the support of our loved ones, our lawyers, our church community, and our fellow immigrants.

JOHNNY ISAKSON
6TH DISTRICT, GEORGIA

EDUCATION AND THE WORKFORCE
WORKFORCE PROTECTIONS
21ST CENTURY COMPETITIVENESS

TRANSPORTATION AND
INFRASTRUCTURE
AVIATION
HIGHWAYS, TRANSIT AND PIPELINES
WATER RESOURCES

Congress of the United States
House of Representatives
Washington, DC 20515–1006
February 16, 2004

WASHINGTON OFFICE:
132 CANNON HOUSE OFFICE BUILDING
WASHINGTON, DC 20515-1006
(202) 225-4501
Fax: (202) 225-4656

DISTRICT OFFICE:
6000 LAKE FORREST DRIVE
SUITE 110
ATLANTA, GA 30328
(404) 252-5239
Fax: (404) 303-1260

http://www.house.gov/isakson

Mr. Eduardo Aguirre
Director
Bureau of Citizenship and Immigration Services
425 I Street, N.W., Room 7030
Washington, D.C. 20536

Charles Kibaara Copy

Dear Mr. Aguirre:

I am writing on behalf of Mr. Charles Nyaga, a resident of my congressional district. It has come to my attention that Mr. Nyaga may be forced to leave the country due solely to backlog at the Immigration & Naturalization Service (INS) and oversight by the Department of Homeland Security (DHS).

In 1996, Mr. Nyaga entered the country on a student visa. The following year, he applied for permanent residence through the diversity visa lottery program and was among those chosen for permanent residence in 1998. Mr. Nyaga turned in all of his paperwork seven months before the September 30, 1998 deadline, however, backlog at the INS prevented his application from being reviewed in time. At the current time, Mr. Nyaga faces expulsion as early as February 20, 2004.

It is truly a disservice that Mr. Nyaga, a man who adhered strictly to our nation's immigration laws, may face deportation because a federal agency did not follow its own timeline and procedures. Mr. Nyaga legally came to America and legally sought to stay in America. Yet we may very well deny him the right to become a citizen because of bureaucratic red tape and senseless oversight. There is something inherently wrong with a system that will punish Mr. Nyaga for following the rules and reward millions of others for breaking them.

I look forward to working with you to resolve Mr. Nyaga's situation and, more importantly, bring about true reform to our immigration system.

Sincerely,

Johnny Isakson
Member of Congress

BCC: Vincent Alig
Henry Hill

51

Chapter Sixteen

"Community Support South minster Presbyterian Church Family"

I immersed myself in the sacred preparations for Sunday services at Southminster Presbyterian Church. My fellow church member Kaye Schuler and I used to prepare for services on Sundays at the church in Marietta. Little did I know that I would gather immense support from my church community.

Within the walls of that sacred place, a congregation rallied behind me, a group of compassionate souls who were determined to see justice served. They tirelessly collected signatures on petitions, supporting my efforts to remain in the country that had become my second home.

My plight had transcended the confines of our church, reaching the ears of influential figures such as Senator Saxby Chambliss, a staunch advocate for my cause. Even federal judges had expressed sympathy for my situation, and I had the rare opportunity to testify before the halls of Congress. Yet, despite the resounding chorus of support, my family and I remained trapped in a seemingly endless legal limbo.

I had not been passive in my pursuit of justice. Alongside Senator Chambliss, I had contributed significantly to the cause. Chambliss, recognizing the injustices faced by individuals like me, introduced a private bill in the U.S. Senate—a silver lining for those whose immigration dreams had been unjustly thwarted.

But our efforts did not end there. Friends contacted the media, shedding light on my story, and the members of my cherished church, Southminster Presbyterian, stood firmly in my corner, speaking passionately in my favor. Their relentless support was the bedrock upon which we stood, for the journey had been arduous and laden with hardships.

My fellow church members were outraged that I might pay the price for the government's inaction. Jan Boehm, a devoted member of Southminster's choir, spoke from the depths of her heart, saying, *"I am so ashamed as an American."* She echoed the sentiments of many who wondered how a nation built on the principles of welcoming the tired and poor could turn its back on those in need.

Driven by their conviction, Southminster Presbyterian and The Cherokee Presbytery members began collecting signatures from fellow churchgoers. They had collected 568 signatures on a petition asking someone - anyone to help me stay in America.

Ms. Boehm had already dispatched 500 signatures to Senator Chambliss, with another hundred, ready for submission in the coming week.

While my supporters fought passionately on my behalf, I reached out to other Georgia legislators, only to be told that Senator Chambliss would be at the forefront of our battle. Time was of the essence, as attorney Charles Kuck rightly pointed out. If legislation were not pending by February 20, we would be forced to face the looming danger of a deportation hearing—a battle that seemed daunting, to say the least.

Kuck, who had been tirelessly advocating for individuals like me trapped in the same bureaucratic mess, expressed his frustration with a system unable to fulfill its duties. *"Immigration simply can't do their job, and these foreign nationals take the brunt of it,"* he said, expressing his concern. Senator Chambliss, however, remained steadfast in his commitment to rectifying the system's flaws. He emphasized, *"The legislation I'm working on solves this problem once and for all, so people in situations like Mr. Nyaga's will not encounter these troubles."*

In the midst of this protracted battle, Senator Chambliss assured us, *"Deportation involves many steps, and we will stay in close contact with the Department of Homeland Security regarding Mr. Nyaga until the situation is resolved."* Once again, our hopes began to surface, but the uncertainty continued to loom over my family.

No matter how hard I tried to put this difficult situation out of my mind and go on with my daily life, it ended up in failure. It interfered sometimes when I tried to do my studies. In the back of your head, it's always there; the worst part is that you can't do anything about it. You can just sit back and wait and hope for the best.

My children were raised in this country and have practically no memories of their homeland. Basically, all of their lives have been here. They're just like every other American teenager. While it's a great achievement that I was able to bring my children here and provide them with a brighter future, it hurts so much to see them having no attachment and memories of the land where they were born.

Me and my wife had tried to keep our boy and girl somewhat shielded from the struggle with immigration authorities though, we talked to them about it. They were concerned, but I don't think they understand the bigger picture.

In the face of these trials, I clung to my faith, a steadfast believer in the tests that life presented. As Christians, we are taught to endure and maintain our faith, even in the most challenging of circumstances. I found peace in my belief in God, viewing this ordeal as a profound test of my faith.

Evil, in various forms, lurked around us, and as followers of Christ, we were called upon to confront it. The battle against evil demanded a vigilant and prepared response. One form of evil I saw creeping into our churches was the acceptance and rationalization of lifestyles that contradicted our values, all in the name of freedom and liberty. Religious groups were cherry-picking scripture verses to justify behaviors that ran counter to our teachings.

The Black Ostrich

Another evil on the rise was religious extremism, which distorted the word of God and radicalized vulnerable youth. These zealous individuals were susceptible to engaging in terrifying acts that threatened the welfare of the society. As Christians, it was our duty not only to pray but also to identify and address these evils and their underlying causes. We needed to return to the sacred texts, study Scripture diligently, and seek answers in God's word.

I recalled a conversation where a grandchild had asked her grandmother why she studied the Bible daily. Her grandmother's response was simple but profound: *"I am studying for my finals."* Indeed, we all had finals to study for, a reminder that our spiritual journey was ongoing, and our faith was the compass that guided us.

I was born into a Christian household, and I was fortunate to have the opportunity to serve at Southminster Presbyterian Church. Throughout my immigration battle, I never felt alone, thanks to the continuous support of my loved ones. With their help, I was able to embark on my journey to become a citizen of my dream country, the United States of America.

Chapter Seventeen

"God Just Showed up
The Most Awaited Day of My Life"

For over a decade, I found myself trapped in an unrelenting coil of administrative red tape and courtroom battles, fighting desperately to rectify a mistake I never made. It was a journey no short of distress and calamities, one that tested my faith. However, amidst these darkest years of my life, unexpected allies emerged in the form of my church family and hardworking attorneys standing right by my side, fighting for my rights.

U.S. Senator Saxby Chambliss, a formidable figure in the political world, threw his weight behind my cause, a powerful advocate for justice. Alongside him stood an army of attorneys and friends, the unsung heroes who tirelessly championed my case. Despite their constant support, the path ahead seemed to darken with the looming shadow of an impending calamity.

I can't recall this event without my eyes welled up. It was almost like God showed up when Atlanta's immigration lawyer, Charles Kuck, made a discovery that would change the course of my fate. He unearthed a hidden gem buried deep within the annals of my case—a family member visa petition filed by my brother Kenneth, a steadfast U.S. citizen, on my behalf back in 1997. This petition had rested in the bureaucratic layers for years, silently awaiting its moment of reckoning.

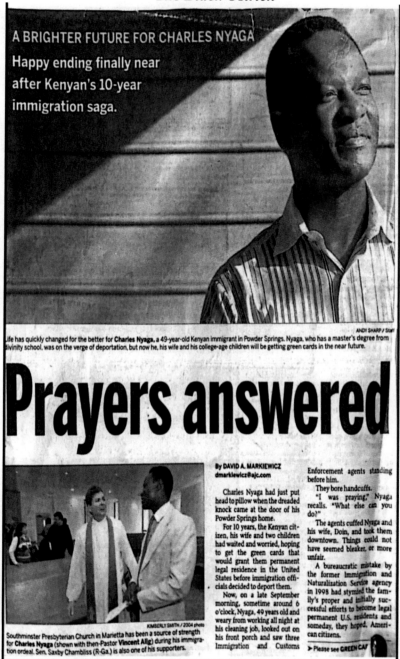

A BRIGHTER FUTURE FOR CHARLES NYAGA

Happy ending finally near after Kenyan's 10-year immigration saga.

ANDY SHARP / Staff

Life has quickly changed for the better for **Charles Nyaga**, a 49-year-old Kenyan immigrant in Powder Springs. Nyaga, who has a master's degree from divinity school, was on the verge of deportation, but now he, his wife and his college-age children will be getting green cards in the near future.

Prayers answered

KIMBERLY SMITH / 2004 photo

Southminster Presbyterian Church in Marietta has been a source of strength for **Charles Nyaga** (shown with then-Pastor **Vincent Allg**) during his immigration ordeal. Sen. Saxby Chambliss (R-Ga.) is also one of his supporters.

By DAVID A. MARKIEWICZ
dmarkiewicz@ajc.com

Charles Nyaga had just put head to pillow when the dreaded knock came at the door of his Powder Springs home.

For 10 years, the Kenyan citizen, his wife and two children had waited and worried, hoping to get the green cards that would grant them permanent legal residence in the United States before immigration officials decided to deport them.

Now, on a late September morning, sometime around 6 o'clock, Nyaga, 49 years old and weary from working all night at his cleaning job, looked out on his front porch and saw three Immigration and Customs Enforcement agents standing before him.

They bore handcuffs.

"I was praying," Nyaga recalls. "What else can you do?"

The agents cuffed Nyaga and his wife, Doin, and took them downtown. Things could not have seemed bleaker, or more unfair.

A bureaucratic mistake by the former Immigration and Naturalization Service agency in 1998 had stymied the family's proper and initially successful efforts to become legal permanent U.S. residents and someday, they hoped, American citizens.

► Please see GREEN CAF

The timing of this revelation was nothing short of miraculous. It presented me with a near-certain path to legal status in the United States, a lifeline cast from the depths of despair. With Kuck's guidance and the surprising collaboration of ICE attorneys, my deportation case was reopened, and an immigration judge halted the proceedings that had threatened to tear my family apart.

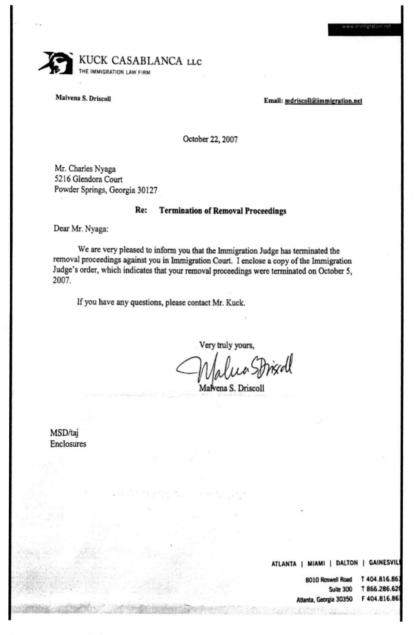

In a matter of days, we transitioned from being forcibly taken from our home in handcuffs to hurtling down the fast track toward obtaining our coveted green cards. It was a breathtaking turnaround, an improbable twist of fate that defied logic and reason. My family's long-awaited moment of legal status was going to happen. I would call it God's work.

Kuck, who had dedicated himself to my cause, confessed his astonishment at the sudden turn of events. *"This,"* he marveled, *"is highly unusual."* He recounted the incredible revelation that had breathed new life into my seemingly hopeless case. *"Charles, you are not going to believe this,"* he told me with a mix of disbelief and jubilation. *"You finally got what you deserved. It's an example of what happens when people work together to help someone."*

The spark for this remarkable transformation ignited during what felt like the darkest hour of our lives. It happened when the Immigration and Customs Enforcement agents descended upon us, ready to enforce our imminent arrest. Yet, in the midst of that turmoil, buried within my case file, one of Kuck's associates stumbled upon the long-forgotten receipt for the family visa application filed by my brother.

"It had become forgotten in the annals of time that this was there," Kuck remarked, reflecting on the astonishing discovery. In contrast, I had carried a vague recollection of its existence in the recesses of my mind, though it had seemed like a distant and unattainable lifeline.

The waiting list for family visas stretched on for years, but remarkably, fate had decided that the application would finally reach the front of the line in October 2007 when Kuck and his team pulled out the dusty file and found that receipt. It was a moment of sheer astonishment. *"Oh my God,"* Kuck exclaimed. *"It was right there."*

The news of this revelation left me skeptical. At that point, our situation had seemed all but irredeemable. However, with the intervention of Senator Chambliss and Kuck's determined efforts, I was released from custody within a day. Lawyers representing ICE cooperated in requesting that my case be reopened, and in October 2007, the immigration judge officially terminated the removal proceedings.

From that moment onward, it was merely a waiting game, with

our green card interview scheduled for March 13, 2008, with the U.S. Bureau of Citizenship and Immigration Services. On that auspicious day, my wife, children, and I received stamps in our passports, marking us as permanent U.S. residents. Soon, our actual green cards would arrive, securing our place in this land of opportunity.

That simple stamp held the promise of a future free from the shackles of immigration uncertainty. It meant that we could live and work in the United States without the constant fear of deportation. With nothing more than a standard green card renewal process standing in our way, we could even aspire to become naturalized citizens in just five years, when the opportunity arose.

"I have rarely seen happier people," Kuck remarked, capturing the joy we experienced as we embarked on this newfound chapter of our lives. My own journey, which had taken me from earning a master's degree from Atlanta's Interdenominational Theological Center to working odd jobs at a local hotel and a cleaning service, was now set on a clear path. I had dreams of pursuing a doctorate or fulfilling my calling as a church pastor or teacher.

Yet, those dreams had remained elusive, obscured by the looming specter of my uncertain visa status. My wife, Doin, a skilled nurse in Kenya, yearned to train as an LPN in the United States. Our college-age children, freed from the weight of our immigration burdens, could finally move forward with their lives, unburdened by the shadows of uncertainty that had haunted us for over a decade.

With over eleven years of battling the system behind us, my family and I could finally think broader toward a better tomorrow. My pursuit of higher education or vocational calling no longer felt like an exercise in futility. Within a span of a few days, it started to feel like our dreams were within reach.

Through it all, I harbored no bitterness, only gratitude for a system that, though flawed, ultimately upheld the rule of law. Senator Chambliss himself recognized the injustice of my situation, labeling it as *"the government's fault"* and affirming my legal status in the country.

Yet, the burden of our immigration struggles had left scars, making us cautious about discussing our experiences in the midst of the impassioned American immigration debate. After all, our story was one of resilience, hope, and triumph, and we had emerged on the other side as stronger, more resilient immigrants who never gave up on their dreams.

It was finally time for my family to move past the looming clouds of doubt and embrace a bright future. Now that I have a master's degree in divinity, I can pursue my goal of becoming a church pastor or teacher without worrying about my visa status. The prospect of starting a new profession in the healthcare industry excited my wife as well, and our kids could now focus on their own goals without having to worry about the immigration issues that had been weighing us down for so long.

For us, it was a victory of faith, endurance, and the conviction that, sometimes, the divine intervention shows up just before the stroke of the twelfth hour.

Chapter Eighteen

"Beyond Labels Embracing Identity and Diversity"

On a fateful day in March 2008, I, along with my family, stepped into the office of the U.S. Bureau of Citizenship and Immigration Services, each one of us carrying our dreams, our hopes, and our aspirations. This interview marked a memorable moment in our lives as we sought a green card to secure our place in the United States of America. While the bureaucratic process was complex, filled with paperwork and interviews, this one time, it was certain that we were going to be green card holders.

We finally got the news we had been waiting for for a few weeks: we would be permanent residents in this diverse and progressive country. It was a historic event that marked the conclusion of years of hard work, commitment, and steadfast faith.

Throughout this journey, one name stood by me and helped me sail through the turbulent sea of immigration bureaucracy—Charles Kuck. He was the embodiment of resilience and determination. He had tirelessly worked day and night to help bring me justice. His constant support and commitment were indispensable, and we owed our success to his dedication.

"I hadn't recalled seeing (the family visa application) before, and he had forgotten about it," Kuck said.

The Black Ostrich

As I ventured into the twists and turns of this immigration ordeal, a strange realization struck me that I hadn't seen the family visa application before. In fact, I had almost forgotten about it. I would have been deported long ago if it weren't for Kuck and Chambliss, who dug out my family visa application filed by my brother.

Another realization I had was amidst these complexities, we had become so entangled that we momentarily lost sight of our roots, origins, and the rich culture of our diverse backgrounds.

In my journey to obtain legal status in the U.S. Senator Saxby Chambliss had appeared as an unexpected ally. The complexities of identity and the celebration of diversity were concepts that resonated with him deeply. During a visit to Washington on April 3, I expressed our heartfelt gratitude to Senator Chambliss for his instrumental role in resolving my case. He recognized that this was a situation where the government was at fault, and I was not.

"I am pleased that Charles' case has been resolved because the problems he encountered were not his fault- this was a case where the government was at fault," Senator Chambliss remarked.

"Charles is a fine individual who is active in his community, and it always makes you feel good to see someone who has come to America for the right reasons, who loves this country, and I certainly wish his family well," he added.

In those words of depth, I found a bridge forming between cultures, a ray of hope that the time is near when the cultural and caste barriers will finally lift and mutual respect and acceptance for all cultures will prevail. Our journey was not just about securing legal status; it was about securing justice for every immigrant who came to the U.S. legally and battling to stay here for the right reasons. It was the battle to bridge the gap between immigrant communities and host countries.

This battle presented us with the chance to tell the world that diversity is beautiful not only because it makes us stronger but also because it brings unique perspectives and ideas, leading to innovation and progress. It is a reminder that we all are different and unique in our own way. We all have something to contribute to this world.

63

Charles

I wish and hope that the world becomes a profoundly accepting space for every individual. By nurturing love, growth, and respect for one another and welcoming each other with open arms to new lands and opportunities, we can make this world a better place for people of all backgrounds.

Chapter Nineteen

"Triumph of the Human Spirit Finding Strength in Unity"

As I'm nearing my retirement, lying on my couch, sipping my coffee, and reminiscing about those times when I fought the biggest battle of life, I cannot help but reflect on the importance of resilience, unity, and unshakeable faith in God. As a Christian, I firmly believe that these are the guiding principles that helped me navigate through those years.

My story is living evidence of the transformative power of these guiding principles and the belief that they can help you achieve anything you set your heart on.

When we strive to make the impossible possible, resilience becomes the lifeblood that flows through our veins, enabling us to climb from the depths of failure to the peaks of glory. Throughout my life, I have faced several challenges, each more formidable than the last. However, what got me through was my unshakeable will and my belief in a greater force. Difficulties of life are rather a blessing that teaches you how to face challenges head-on, no matter how hopeless they may appear. They serve as a constant determination to move forward, adjust, overcome, and come out stronger.

Charles

As immigrants, we frequently deal with strange environments, take on unfamiliar challenges, and venture into the lanes we have never been to. Our greatest power at these times is our solidarity. When we stand shoulder to shoulder, we emerge stronger and unstoppable. Our solidarity creates a close-knit support system that gets us through life's ups and downs. It's the comforting embrace of loved ones who are aware of the difficulties we endure. It's the relationships we develop with other immigrants, brought together by a similar path and aspiration.

My firm faith in God has helped me sail through the stormy seas of life. It has given me comfort and strength when I've been feeling doubtful and hopeless. It's the conviction that there is a higher purpose behind everything that happens, even in the midst of chaos. Faith teaches us that every event has something to teach us and that every setback presents an opportunity for improvement. We are given the strength to endure because we are aware that we are not alone.

Among the most valuable lessons I've learned are the significance of adaptation and self-transformation. We must frequently let go of our old selves in order to grow and welcome new situations with an open mind and an open heart. I have personally experienced firsthand the amazing ability to adjust to changing circumstances. It's the readiness to leave one's comfort zone and face uncertainty. It's an acknowledgment that personal development is a lifelong process and a dedication to lifelong learning and self-improvement.

As immigrants, we occasionally encounter prejudice and bigotry. We must try to approach this terrible reality with optimism. Breaking down barriers can be facilitated by responding to ignorance and prejudice with grace and education. It's about showcasing our cultures, telling our stories, and demonstrating to the outside world how our uniqueness makes us so incredibly varied. By addressing prejudices with compassion and empathy, we create unifying bonds that will last forever.

Chapter Twenty

"Never Give Up: My Message to Immigrants Facing Deportation"

"Sit with Charles Nyaga in his living room, and everything seems fine.

The sun shines through the windows of his modest Powder Springs home, casting family photos in a warm light and bathing his face in a serene slow.

Mention his "situation," though, and his expression turns dark.

Wearily, softly, in the lilting cadence of his native Kenya, he tries to explain how it feels to go from invited guest to intruder in the eyes of the federal government - through no fault of his own.

The 49-year-old aspiring pastor legally came to the United States from Kenya a decade ago. He has been trying ever since to gain legal residency - and eventually citizenship - but federal immigration authorities have threatened to expel him for a mistake they made," wrote David A. Markiewicz.

Reflecting on my journey, I realized I was not alone in my struggle to remain in the United States. It was no longer my fight alone; it was a fight for every immigrant who came here legally and faced deportation due to bureaucratic errors.

I know of a few others who were in the same situation as I was because of government inaction. We all followed the rules but nonetheless faced deportation. For example, a Swiss national who was in the US as an investor before being selected as a winner under the Diversity Visa Lottery program had to sell his business because the Immigration Service did not process his green card in time. A South African airline pilot whose application for permanent residence was not timely adjudicated ended up losing his job because of the failure to process his application in a timely manner. A Russian national whose wife is a lawful permanent resident will now have to wait back in Russia for several years while she awaits her naturalization to be approved. All of these individuals, as well as countless hundreds or perhaps thousands more, have been victimized by the inaction of the Immigration Service and the erroneous and incomplete instructions of the Department of State, which notifies the "winners."

Therefore, people who have done everything our government requires of us to do, through no fault of their own, ultimately are unable to become permanent residents under the Diversity Visa Program. I am fortunate that my family and I have not had to face this situation alone. My family, attorneys, and the members of my church have stood by me in every way possible. I want to take this opportunity to publicly thank them from the bottom of my heart.

I am also very grateful to Senator Saxby Chambliss (R-GA), the chair of the Senate Subcommittee on Immigration, Border Security, and Citizenship, for introducing legislation, S. 2089, that addressed my situation. This targeted legislation provided welcome relief to people like myself and my family, and others who, during fiscal years 1998 through 2003, were unable to obtain permanent residence under the DV program because the fiscal year ended before their cases were approved. The bill authorized such individuals to reopen their cases and continue processing as long as diversity visas for the fiscal year in which they filed remain available.

I hope the government will introduce more such legislation to help immigrants legally obtain their permanent residence in the US promptly. It was the positive efforts of Senator Chambliss and the other members of the Senate who supported individuals such as myself, who had been deprived of the legal benefit of permanent residence by the inaction of the former Immigration Service.

Law-abiding people who follow the rules, pay the required fees, and rely on the government's procedures should not be punished because of government inaction.

In closing, I urge all immigrants who have come to the United States legally and with a genuine purpose to stay strong, resilient, and hopeful. No one can force you to leave, but you must never give up on your goal of becoming a permanent resident.

Charles

Made in the USA
Columbia, SC
10 July 2024

fb4cb349-58c2-4da9-b200-d5eb731b7ebfR01